The Christian Children's SONGBOOK

ISBN 0-634-00336-4

HAL•LEONARD®
CORPORATION
7777 W. BLUEMOUND RD. P.O. BOX 13819 MILWAUKEE, WI 53213

Visit Hal Leonard Online at
www.halleonard.com

Contents

ALIVE, ALIVE

Traditional

ALL NIGHT, ALL DAY

Traditional Spiritual

Day is dy-in' in ___ the west,
Now I lay me down ___ to sleep,

An - gels watch-in' o - ver me, my Lord. ___ Sleep, my child, and
An - gels watch-in' o - ver me, my Lord. ___ Pray the Lord my

take ___ your rest, An - gels watch-in' o - ver me.
soul ___ to keep, An - gels watch-in' o - ver me.

THE BUTTERFLY SONG
(If I Were a Butterfly)

Words and Music by
BRIAN HOWARD

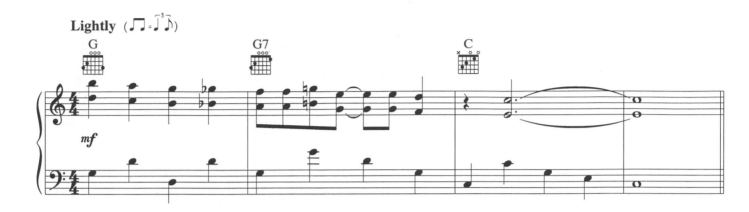

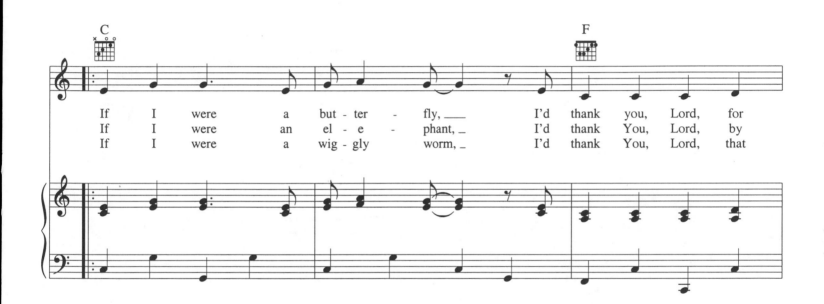

If I were a but-ter - fly, ___ I'd thank you, Lord, for
If I were an el - e - phant, _ I'd thank You, Lord, by
If I were a wig - gly worm, _ I'd thank You, Lord, that

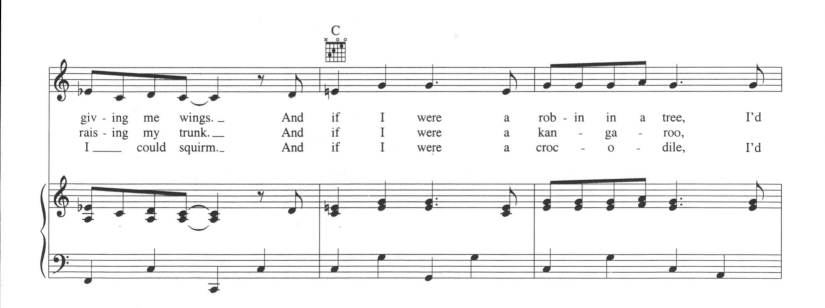

giv - ing me wings. _ And if I were a rob - in in a tree, I'd
rais - ing my trunk. _ And if I were a kan - ga - roo,
I ___ could squirm. _ And if I were a croc - o - dile, I'd

ALL THINGS BRIGHT AND BEAUTIFUL

Words by CECIL FRANCES ALEXANDER
17th Century English Melody
Arranged by MARTIN SHAW

ARKY, ARKY

Traditional

Brightly

1. The Lord ___ told No-ah, there's gon-na be a flood-y, flood-y,
2.-5.(See additional lyrics)

Lord ___ told No-ah, there's gon-na be a flood-y, flood-y, Get those an-i-mals

out of the mud-dy, mud-dy, chil-dren of the Lord. So

Chorus

Additional Lyrics

2. The Lord told Noah to build him an arky, arky,
Lord told Noah to build him an arky, arky,
Build it out of gopher barky, barky,
Children of the Lord.
Chorus

3. The animals, the animals, they came in by twosies, twosies,
Animals, the animals, they came in by twosies, twosies,
Elephants and kangaroosies, roosies,
Children of the Lord.
Chorus

4. It rained and poured for forty daysies, daysies,
Rained and poured for forty daysies, daysies,
Almost drove those animals crazies, crazies,
Children of the Lord.
Chorus

5. The sun came out and dried up the landy, landy,
(Look, there's the sun!) It dried up the landy, landy,
Everything was fine and dandy, dandy,
Children of the Lord.
Chorus

AWESOME GOD

Words and Music by
RICH MULLINS

BEHOLD, WHAT MANNER OF LOVE

Words and Music by
PATRICIA VAN TINE

With a lilt

*Part I **

Be -

hold, what man - ner of love the Fa - ther has

giv - en un - to us, _____ be - hold, what man - ner of

* May be sung as a two-part round.

THE B-I-B-L-E

Traditional

Word of God, the B - I - B - L -

E. The B - I - B - L -

E.

THE BIBLE TELLS ME SO

Words and Music by
DALE EVANS

CLAP YOUR HANDS

Words and Music by JIMMY OWENS
Text Based on Psalm 47:1

Clap your hands, all you peo-ple.

Shout un-to God with a voice of tri-umph.

Clap your hands, all you peo-ple.

CLIMB UP SUNSHINE MOUNTAIN

Words and Music by
V.O. FOSSETT

Climb, climb up sun - shine moun - tain,
heav'n - ly breez - es blow. Climb, climb up
sun - shine moun - tain, fac - es all a -

COME INTO HIS PRESENCE
(Singing Alleluia)

Unknown

Lyrics:

Come in-to His pres-ence sing-ing {
Al - le - lu - ia, Al - le - lu - ia,
Je - sus is Lord, Je - sus is Lord,
}

1. Al - le - lu - ia.
2. Je - sus is Lord

Praise the Lord to-geth-er sing-ing

{
Wor - thy the Lamb, Wor - thy the Lamb,
Glo - ry to God, Glo - ry to God,
}

Wor - thy the Lamb.

Glo - ry to God.

CREATURE PRAISE

Words and Music by
DAVID MATTHEWS

DARE TO BE A DANIEL

Words and Music by
PHILIP P. BLISS

DAY BY DAY
from the Musical GODSPELL

Words and Music by
STEPHEN SCHWARTZ

Easy Waltz feel

Day by day,_____ Day by day,_____

Oh, dear Lord,_____ three things I pray_____

to see Thee more clear-ly, love Thee more dear-ly,

DEEP AND WIDE

Traditional

Moderately

mf

Deep and wide, deep and wide, There's a foun- tain flow-ing deep and wide.

Deep and wide, deep and wide, There's a foun- tain flow-ing deep and wide.

foun- tain flow-ing, there's a foun- tain flow-ing, there's a foun- tain flow-ing deep and wide.

DO LORD

Traditional

DOWN IN MY HEART

Traditional

EVERY TIME I FEEL THE SPIRIT

African-American Spiritual

FATHER ABRAHAM

Traditional

Lyrics:

Fa-ther A-bra-ham had man-y sons, and man-y sons had Fa-ther A-bra-ham. I am one of them and so are you, so let's just praise the Lord, *right arm. Fa-ther Lord, right arm, left

* *Start a continuous motion with the right arm. Add a motion each time a new part of the body is mentioned.*

GIVE ME OIL IN MY LAMP

Traditional

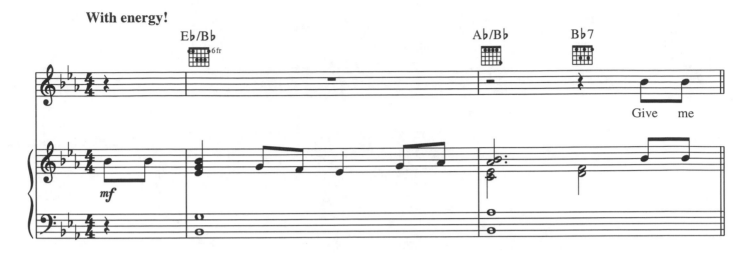

FATHER I ADORE YOU

Words and Music by
TERRY COELHO STROM

* *May be sung as a three-part round.*

FISHERS OF MEN

Words and Music by
HARRY D. CLARKE

FOR THE BEAUTY OF THE EARTH

Words by FOLLIOT S. PIERPOINT
Music by CONRAD KOCHER

round us lies.
thoughts and mild;
Christ, our God, to Thee we raise
Lord of all, to Thee we raise

this our hymn of grate - ful praise.
this our sac - ri - fice of praise.

For the __ beau - ty
For Thy __ church that

of each hour
ev - er - more
of the day and
lift - eth ho - ly
of the night,
hands a - bove,

* for Holy Communion

GIVE THANKS

Words and Music by
HENRY SMITH

GLORIFY THY NAME

Words and Music by
DONNA ADKINS

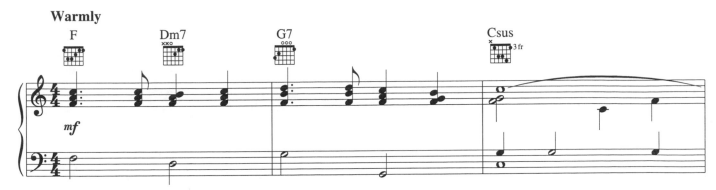

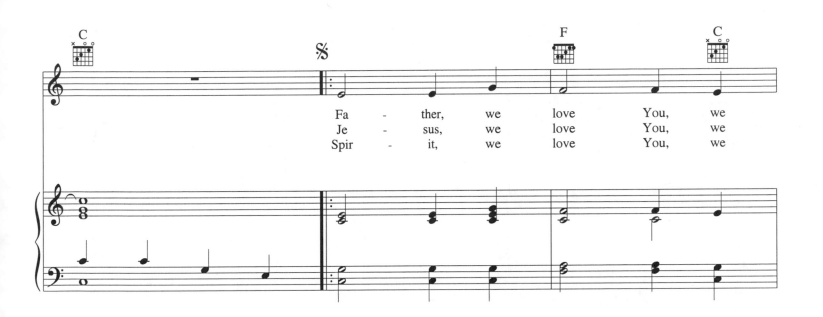

Fa - ther, we love You, we
Je - sus, we love You, we
Spir - it, we love You, we

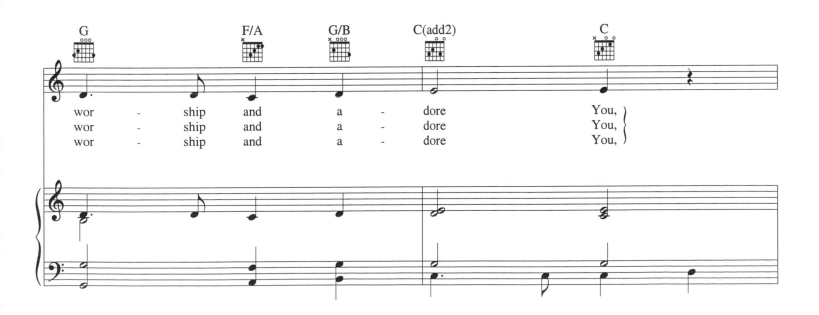

wor - ship and a - dore You,
wor - ship and a - dore You,
wor - ship and a - dore You,

GLORY BE TO GOD ON HIGH

Traditional

GOD IS SO GOOD

Traditional

THE GOSPEL TRAIN

African-American Spiritual

GREAT DAY

Traditional Spiritual

8vb

GREAT IS THE LORD

Words and Music by MICHAEL W. SMITH
and DEBORAH D. SMITH

HALLELU, HALLELUJAH!

Traditional

Hal - le - lu, hal - le - lu, hal - le - lu, hal - le - lu - jah! Praise ye the Lord! Hal - le - lu, hal - le - lu, hal - le - lu, hal - le - lu - jah! Praise ye the Lord! Praise ye the Lord! Hal - le - lu - jah! Praise ye the

HE HAS MADE ME GLAD

By LEONA VON BRETHORST

I will en-ter His gates with thanks-giv-ing in my heart, I will en-ter His courts with praise.

HE'S GOT THE WHOLE WORLD
IN HIS HANDS

Traditional Spiritual

HOW MAJESTIC IS YOUR NAME

Words and Music by
MICHAEL W. SMITH

HE'S STILL WORKIN' ON ME

Words and Music by
JOEL HEMPHILL

HIS BANNER OVER ME IS LOVE

Text based on Song Of Solomon 2:4, 16
Traditional Music

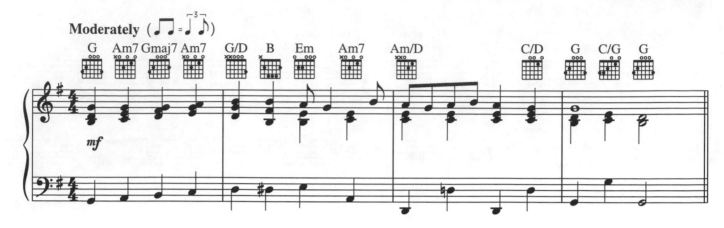

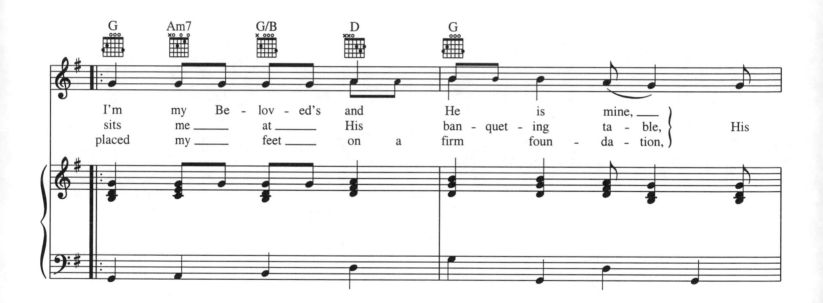

I'm my Be-lov-ed's and He is mine,

sits me ___ at ___ His ban-quet-ing ta-ble, His

placed my ___ feet ___ on a firm foun-da-tion,

ban-ner o-ver me is love.

He sits me ___ at ___ His

He placed my ___ feet ___ on a

I'm my Be-lov-ed's and

HO-HO-HO-HOSANNA

Traditional

HOSANNA! HOSANNA!

Words and Music by
HELEN KEMP

I AM A C-H-R-I-S-T-I-A-N

Traditional

I AM A PROMISE

Words by WILLIAM J. GAITHER and GLORIA GAITHER
Music by WILLIAM J. GAITHER

I LOVE YOU LORD

Words and Music by
LAURIE KLEIN

I love You, Lord, _____ and I

lift my voice _____ to wor - ship You. O my

I WILL SING OF THE MERCIES
(Of the Lord)

Words based on Psalm 89:1
Music by JAMES H. FILLMORE

I'LL BE A SUNBEAM

Words by NELLIE TALBOT
Music by EDWIN O. EXCELL

I'M GONNA SING, SING, SING

Traditional

With energy!

mf

I'm gon-na sing, sing, sing. I'm gon-na

shout, shout, shout. I'm gon-na sing, I'm gon-na

shout, "Praise the Lord!" When those

I'M IN THE LORD'S ARMY

Traditional

I'M GONNA SING WHEN THE SPIRIT SAYS SING

African-American Spiritual

I'm gon - na sing when the Spir - it says sing, I'm gon - na
shout when the Spir - it says shout, I'm gon - na

sing when the Spir - it says sing. __ I'm gon - na sing when the Spir - it says
shout when the Spir - it says shout. __ I'm gon - na shout when the Spir - it says

sing, } and o - bey the Spir - it of the Lord. I'm gon - na
shout, }

I'VE GOT PEACE LIKE A RIVER

Traditional

IF YOU'RE HAPPY
AND YOU KNOW IT

Words and Music by
L. SMITH

INTO MY HEART

Words and Music by
HARRY D. CLARKE

IS THERE ANYTHING I CAN DO FOR YOU?

Words and Music by DOTTIE RAMBO
and DAVID HUNTSINGER

JACOB'S LADDER

African-American Spiritual

JESUS BIDS US SHINE

Words by SUSAN WARNER
Music by EDWIN EXCELL

JESUS IN THE MORNING

Traditional

JESUS LOVES EVEN ME

(I Am So Glad)

Words and Music by
PHILIP P. BLISS

JESUS LOVES ME

Words by ANNA B. WARNER
Music by WILLIAM B. BRADBURY

Je - sus loves me! This I know, For the Bi - ble tells me so.
Je - sus loves me, He who died, Heav - en's gate to o - pen wide.

Lit - tle ones to Him be - long; They are weak, but He is strong.
He will wash a - way my sin, Let his lit - tle child come in.

Yes, Je - sus loves me! ___ Yes, Je - sus loves me! ___ Yes, Je - sus

JESUS LOVES THE LITTLE CHILDREN

Words by REV. C.H. WOOLSTON
Music by GEORGE F. ROOT

JOSHUA
(Fit the Battle of Jericho)

African-American Spiritual

Josh-ua fit the bat-tle of ___ Jer-i-cho, ___ Jer-i-cho, ___

Jer-i-cho, _____ Lord, __ Josh-ua fit the bat-tle of ___

Jer-i-cho __ and the walls come tum-blin' down.

THE JOY OF THE LORD

Text Based on Nehemiah 8:10
Music by ALLIENE G. VALE

KING OF KINGS

Words and Music by SOPHIE CONTY
and NAOMI YAH

KUM BA YAH

Traditional Spiritual

LET THERE BE PEACE ON EARTH

Words and Music by SY MILLER
and JILL JACKSON

LITTLE DAVID, PLAY ON YOUR HARP

Traditional

LORD, I WANT TO BE A CHRISTIAN

Traditional Spiritual

LORD, BE GLORIFIED

Words and Music by
BOB KILPATRICK

LOVE IS

Words and Music by
DOTTIE RAMBO

Simply

Love is a ver- y spe-cial thing, A smile, a tear, a soft sum-mer rain. It

has no be - gin - ning, it has no end, but

I like it best when it's shared with a friend.

friend.

I like it best when it's shared with a friend.

MICHAEL, ROW THE BOAT ASHORE

Traditional Folksong

Mi - chael, row _____ the boat a - shore, hal - le -
lu - jah. Mi - chael, row the boat a -
shore, hal - le - lu - jah.
1. Sis - ter,
2. Jor - dan
3. Jor - dan

MY GOD IS SO GREAT, SO STRONG AND SO MIGHTY

Traditional

NO WAY, WE ARE NOT ASHAMED

Words and Music by
CARMAN

NOTHING BUT THE BLOOD

Words and Music by
ROBERT LOWRY

Additional Lyrics

2.   For my pardon this I see
     Nothing but the blood of Jesus;
     For my cleansing this my plea
     Nothing but the blood of Jesus.
     Refrain

3.   Nothing can for sin atone
     Nothing but the blood of Jesus;
     Naught of good that I have done
     Nothing but the blood of Jesus.
     Refrain

O HOW HE LOVES YOU AND ME

Words and Music by
KURT KAISER

Lyrics:

O how He loves you and me! O how He loves you and me! He gave His life, what more could He give?

PASS IT ON

Words and Music by
KURT KAISER

OH, BE CAREFUL

Traditional

OH, HOW I LOVE JESUS

Words by FREDERICK WHITFIELD
Traditional American Melody

There is a name __ I love to hear, I love to sing __ its worth; __ It sounds like mu - sic in my ear, the sweet - est name on earth. __ Oh, how I love Je - sus, Oh, how I love

PRAISE HIM, ALL YE LITTLE CHILDREN

Traditional Words
Music by CAREY BONNER

PRAISE THE NAME OF JESUS

Words and Music by
ROY HICKS, JR.

PUT YOUR HAND IN THE HAND

Words and Music by
GENE MacLELLAN

REDEEMED

Words by FANNY J. CROSBY
Music by A.L. BUTLER

REJOICE IN THE LORD ALWAYS

Words from Philippians 4:4
Traditional Music

May be sung as a four-part round (2x).

ROCK-A-MY SOUL

African-American Spiritual

SAY TO THE LORD, "I LOVE YOU"

Words and Music by
ERNIE RETTINO

Touch your fin - ger to your nose,
Reach your hands up to the sky,

bend from the waist way down and touch your toes. And when you
look to the left, then down right and blink your eyes. And when you

come up slow - ly, start to _____ sing,
turn a - round, you'll start to _____ sing,
And

SEEK YE FIRST

Words and Music by
KAREN LAFFERTY

SIMPLE GIFTS

Traditional Shaker Hymn

Warmly

'Tis a gift to be sim-ple, 'tis a gift to be free, 'tis a gift to come down where you ought to be, and when we find our-selves in the

SIYAHAMBA
(We Are Marching in the Light of God)

African Folksong

Pronunciation Guide

Siyahamba = see-yah-hahm-bah
Ekukha = eh-koo-kah
Nyeni = n͜yeh-nee
Kwenkhos' = kwehn-kōs

STANDIN' IN THE NEED OF PRAYER

African-American Spiritual

THE STEADFAST LOVE OF THE LORD

Words and Music by
EDITH McNEILL

STOP! AND LET ME TELL YOU

Traditional

TELL ME THE STORIES OF JESUS

Words by WILLIAM H. PARKER
Music by FREDERIC A. CHALLINOR

THERE IS A REDEEMER

Words and Music by
MELODY GREEN

1. There is a re - deem - er,

2.-4. *(See additional lyrics)*

Je - sus, God's own Son. _____

Additional Lyrics

2. **Jesus, my redeemer,**
   Name above all names.
   Precious Lamb of God, Messiah,
   Oh, for sinners slain. *(To Chorus)*

3. **When I stand in glory,**
   I will see His face,
   And there I'll serve my King forever
   In that holy place. *(To Chorus)*

4. **There is a redeemer,**
   Jesus, God's own Son.
   Precious Lamb of God, Messiah,
   Holy One. *(To Chorus)*

TELL ME THE STORY OF JESUS

Words by FANNY J. CROSBY
Music by JOHN R. SWENEY

THIS IS MY FATHER'S WORLD

Words by MALTBIE BABCOCK
Music by FRANKLIN L. SHEPPARD

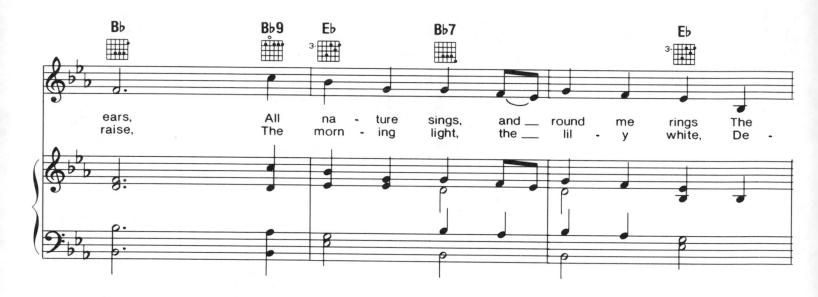

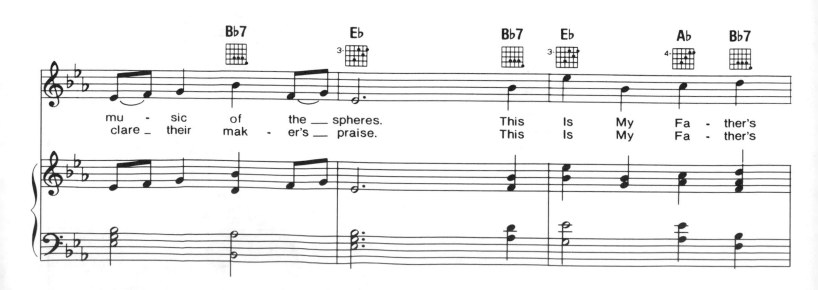

THIS LITTLE LIGHT OF MINE

African-American Spiritual

THIS IS THE DAY

By LES GARRETT

THIS LITTLE LIGHT OF MINE
(2nd Tune)

Traditional

I'm gon-na let it shine, let it shine, let it shine, let it shine, let it shine!

shine!

THY WORD

Words and Music by MICHAEL W. SMITH
and AMY GRANT

Moderately, flowing

Thy Word is a lamp un-to ___ my feet and a light un-to my path.

Thy Word is a lamp un-to ___ my feet and a

WE ARE THE REASON

Words and Music by
DAVID MEECE

241

WHAT A MIGHTY GOD WE SERVE

Traditional

WHEN THE SAINTS GO MARCHING IN

Words by KATHERINE E. PURVIS
Music by JAMES M. BLACK

THE WISE MAN AND THE FOOLISH MAN

Traditional

ZACCHAEUS

Traditional

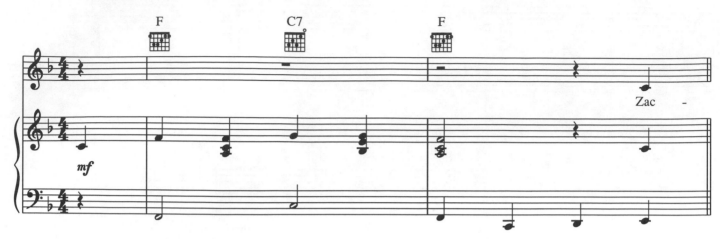

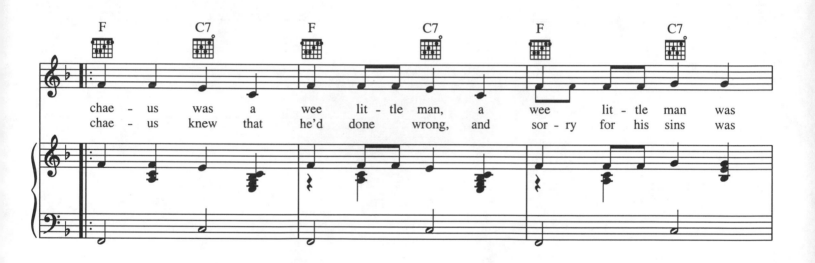

Lord he want-ed to see. And as the Sav- ior
all my goods," ed said he. "And if I've cheat - ed

passed that way, he looked up in the tree, *and He said, "Zacchaeus, you come down, for* I'm
an - y - one, four times will I re - pay." *and Jesus said, "Salvation has come to you!* I have

go - ing to your house to - day, for I'm
come ___ to ___ seek and save. I have

1
go - ing to your house to - day, Zac -
come __ to ___ seek and

2
save."

THY WORD HAVE I HID IN MY HEART

Text based on Psalm 119:11
Music by EARNEST O. SELLERS

The Finest Inspirational Music

Songbooks arranged for piano, voice, and guitar.

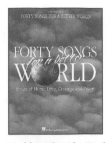

40 SONGS FOR A BETTER WORLD

40 songs with a message, including: All You Need Is Love • Bless The Beasts And Children • Colors Of The Wind • Everything Is Beautiful • He Ain't Heavy...He's My Brother • I Am Your Child • Love Can Build A Bridge • What A Wonderful World • What The World Needs Now Is Love • You've Got A Friend • and more.
00310096......................$15.95

BEST GOSPEL SONGS EVER

80 of the best-loved Gospel songs of all time, including: Amazing Grace • At Calvary • Because He Lives • Behold the Lamb • Daddy Sang Bass • Get All Excited • His Eye Is on the Sparrow • I Saw the Light • I'd Rather Have Jesus • I'll Fly Away • Just a Little Talk With Jesus • Mansion Over the Hilltop • My Tribute • Precious Lord, Take My Hand • and more.
00310503......................$19.95

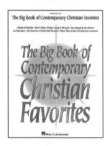

BIG BOOK OF CONTEMPORARY CHRISTIAN FAVORITES

A comprehensive collection of 50 songs, including: Angels • El Shaddai • Friends • The Great Adventure • I Will Be Here • Love In Any Language • Love Will Be Our Home • O Magnify The Lord • People Need The Lord • Say The Name • Turn Up The Radio • Via Dolorosa • Whatever You Ask • Where There Is Faith • and more.
00310021......................$19.95

CONTEMPORARY CHRISTIAN VOCAL GROUP FAVORITES

15 songs, including: The Basics Of Life • A Few Good Men • The Great Divide • Undivided • and more.

00310019......................$10.95

CONTEMPORARY CHRISTIAN WEDDING SONGBOOK

30 appropriate songs for weddings, including: Household Of Faith • Love In Any Language • Love Will Be Our Home • Parents' Prayer • This Is Love • Where There Is Love • and more.
00310022......................$14.95

COUNTRY/GOSPEL U.S.A.

50 songs written for piano/guitar/four-part vocal. Highlights: An American Trilogy • Daddy Sang Bass • He Set Me Free • I Saw The Light • I'll Meet You In The Morning • Kum Ba Yah • Mansion Over The Hilltop • Love Lifted Me • Turn Your Radio On • When The Saints Go Marching In • many more.
00240139......................$9.95

EXALT HIS NAME!

23 contemporary Christian favorites, including: Easter Song • A Few Good Men • For The Sake Of The Call • The Great Adventure • Heaven In The Real World • Keep My Mind • Say The Name • Serve The Lord • Wise Up • and more.
00310101......................$14.95

FAVORITE HYMNS

An outstanding collection of 71 all-time favorites, including: Abide With Me • Amazing Grace • Ave Maria • Bringing In The Sheaves • Christ The Lord Is Risen Today • Crown Him With Many Crowns • Faith Of Our Fathers • He's Got The Whole World In His Hands • In The Sweet By And By • Jesus Loves Me! • Just A Closer Walk With Thee • Kum Ba Yah • A Mighty Fortress Is Our God • Onward Christian Soldiers • Rock Of Ages • Swing Low, Sweet Chariot • Were You There? • and many more!
00490436......................$12.95

GREAT HYMNS TREASURY

A comprehensive collection of 70 favorites: Close To Thee • Footsteps Of Jesus • Amazing Grace • At The Cross • Blessed Assurance • Blest Be The Tie That Binds • Church In The Wildwood • The Church's One Foundation • God Of Our Fathers • His Eye Is On The Sparrow • How Firm A Foundation • I Love To Tell The Story • In The Garden • It Is Well With My Soul • Just A Closer Walk With Thee • Just As I Am • Nearer My God, To Thee • Now That We All Our God • The Old Rugged Cross • The Lily Of The Valley • We're Marching To Zion • Were You There? • What A Friend We Have In Jesus • When I Survey The Wondrous Cross • and more.
00310167......................$12.95

THE NEW YOUNG MESSIAH

Matching folio to the album featuring today's top contemporary Christian artists performing a modern rendition of Handel's *Messiah*. Features Sandy Patty, Steven Curtis Chapman, Larnelle Harris, and others.
00310006......................$16.95

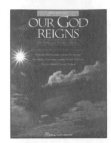

OUR GOD REIGNS

A collection of over 70 songs of praise and worship, including: El Shaddai • Find Us Faithful • His Eyes • Holy Ground • How Majestic Is Your Name • Proclaim The Glory Of The Lord • Sing Your Praise To The Lord • Thy Word • and more.
00311695......................$17.95

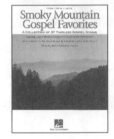

SMOKY MOUNTAIN GOSPEL FAVORITES

37 favorites, including: Amazing Grace • At Calvary • At The Cross • Blessed Assurance • Church In The Wildwood• I Love To Tell The Story • In The Garden • In The Sweet By And By • The Old Rugged Cross • Rock Of Ages • Shall We Gather At The River • Softly And Tenderly • Tell It To Jesus • Wayfaring Stranger • We're Marching To Zion • What A Friend We Have In Jesus • When The Roll Is Called Up Yonder • When We All Get to Heaven • and more.
00310161......................$8.95

ULTIMATE GOSPEL – 100 SONGS OF DEVOTION

Includes: El Shaddai • His Eye Is On The Sparrow • How Great Thou Art • Just A Closer Walk With Thee • Lead Me, Guide Me • (There'll Be) Peace In The Valley (For Me) • Precious Lord, Take My Hand • Wings Of A Dove • more.

00241009......................$19.95

FOR MORE INFORMATION, SEE YOUR LOCAL MUSIC DEALER, OR WRITE TO:

HAL•LEONARD® CORPORATION
7777 W. BLUEMOUND RD. P.O. BOX 13819 MILWAUKEE, WI 53213

Visit us on-line at halleonard.com for a complete listing of titles.

0699